All the Best

The Selected Poems of
Roger McGough

Illustrated by Lydia Monks

PUFFIN

PUFFIN BOOKS

Published by the Penguin Group
Penguin Books Ltd, 80 Strand, London WC2R 0RL, England
Penguin Group (USA), Inc., 375 Hudson Street, New York, New York 10014, USA
Penguin Books Australia Ltd, 250 Camberwell Road, Camberwell, Victoria 3124, Australia
Penguin Books Canada Ltd, 10 Alcorn Avenue, Toronto, Ontario, Canada M4V 3B2
Penguin Books India (P) Ltd, 11 Community Centre, Panchsheel Park, New Delhi – 110 017, India
Penguin Group (NZ), cnr Airborne and Rosedale Roads, Albany, Auckland 1310, New Zealand
Penguin Books (South Africa) (Pty) Ltd, 24 Sturdee Avenue, Rosebank 2196, South Africa

Penguin Books Ltd, Registered Offices: 80 Strand, London WC2R 0RL, England

www.penguin.com

First published in hardback 2003
First published in paperback 2004
1 3 5 7 9 10 8 6 4 2

Text copyright © Roger McGough, 2003
Illustrations copyright © Lydia Monks, 2003
All rights reserved

The moral right of the author and illustrator has been asserted

Set in Centaur MT

Made and printed in China by Midas Printing Ltd.

British Library Cataloguing in Publication Data
A CIP catalogue record for this book is available from the British Library

ISBN 0–141–31637–3

Contents

The Writer of This Poem   1

The Reader of This Poem   2

First Day at School   4

What I Love About School   6

Head   8

Class Warfare   9

Mums and Dads   10

The Leader   12

The Boy with a Similar Name   13

It Wasn't Me, Miss   16

Streemin   17

Harum Scarum   18

Butterfingers   18

Easy Money   19

Reward and Punishment   20

Plague Around   22

Riddle   23

The Magic Pebble   24

My Brilliant Friend   25

A Good Poem   26

A Great Poem 27

Apostrophe 28

Watchwords 29

Smithereens 30

The Power of Poets 31

A Poem Just For Me 32

The Super-Word Market 33

Choose the Rhyme 33

Waxing Lyrical 34

I Wish I Were a Crochet 36

The All-Purpose Children's Poem 37

The Cackle 38

No Grannies in This Poem 39

Pillow Talk 40

I've Taken to My Bed 42

Wink 42

Top 43

The Missing Sock 44

I've Got a Cold 44

Wouldn't It Be Funny If You Didn't Have a Nose? 46

Hide and Seek 48

Itch 48

Tantrums 48

Bottom   49

Sky in the Pie!   50

The Burp   52

Lollidollops   53

Bun Fight   54

No Peas For the Wicked   55

Keep Your Eyes Peeled   56

Cabbage   56

Vegetarians   57

'US Flies in Hamburgers'   58

A Weak Poem   59

The Fight of the Year   60

Autumn Poem   62

First Haiku of Spring   62

Trees Are Great   63

Why Trees Have Got It All Wrong   64

Storm   65

The Snowman   66

Haiku   67

Snow and Ice Poems   68

The Midnight Skaters   70

In Good Hands   71

Downhill Racer   72

Uphill Climb   73

Pinning up a Notice 74

Mrs Moon 75

Icy Fingers 75

The Sad Astronomer 76

Mad Ad 77

One More Battle 78

Give and Take 79

Five-Car Family 80

Everything Touches 82

Borrowed Time 83

Eye Sore 83

Estate 84

Neighbourhood Watch 84

Fire Guard 85

Zebra Crossing 85

I Say I Say I Say 86

A Cat, a Horse and the Sun 87

Pussy Pussy Puddle Cat 88

Marmalade 88

The Cats' Protection League 89

Mafia Cats 90

Cousin Reggie 92

Cousin Nell 93

Uncle Terry 94

Eno	95
All's Well That Ends	96
Cautionary Tale	97
Moany Margaret	100
Bucket	102
Strangeways	103
Blue Macaw	104
Wiwis	105
Ostrich	105
Crow	106
Seagulls	107
Love a Duck	108
Why Do Sheep	109
A Domesticated Donkey	109
Poor Old Dead Horses	110
Hundreds and Thousands	111
Said the Water Boatman	112
A Porcupine	113
Pull the Other One	114
Goldfish	115
Didgeridoo	116
Ticklish	117
Handfish	118
Whales	119

Cross Porpoises   120

A Conger Eel   120

Old Hippos   121

Poor Old Moose   122

Shark in the Park   123

Crocodile Farm   123

The Allivator   125

An Anaconda   126

A Water Bison   126

A Teapet   127

A Catapillow   128

A 13-Amp Slug   128

The Brushbaby   129

Bookworms   130

A War Thog   131

Born to Bugle   132

Bubble Trouble   134

Good Mates   135

Me and My Shadow   136

A Gottle of Geer   137

Potato Clock   138

Simple Questions   139

Zombie   146

The Going Pains   147

A Ring   148

What She Did   150

Joy at the Sound   151

Fame   152

Superman's Little Brother   153

Goodbat Nightman   154

The Figment Tree   155

When to Cut Your Fingernails   156

Tears For the Tooth Fairy   157

Gruesome   158

Film   159

Cling-Film   159

The Scarecrow   160

Only a Dream?   162

Pantomime Poem   163

Customer Service   164

I'm a Grown Man Now   164

Limps   165

The Kleptomaniac   166

The Man Who Steals Dreams   168

The Tongue-twister   169

The Sound Collector   170

Lullaby   172

The Writer of This Poem

The writer of this poem
Is taller than a tree
As keen as the North wind
As handsome as can be

As bold as a boxing glove
As sharp as a nib
As strong as scaffolding
As tricky as a fib

As smooth as an ice cream
As quick as a lick
As clean as a chemist shop
As clever as a ✓

The writer of this poem
Never ceases to amaze
He's one in a million billion
(or so the poem says!)

The Reader of This Poem

The reader of this poem
Is as cracked as a cup
As daft as treacle toffee
As mucky as a pup

As troublesome as bubblegum
As brash as a brush
As bouncy as a double-tum
As quiet as a sshhh . . .

As sneaky as a witch's spell
As tappy-toe as jazz
As empty as a wishing-well
As echoey as as as as as as . . . as . . . as . . .

As bossy as a whistle
As prickly as a pair
Of boots made out of thistles
And elephant hair

As vain as trainers
As boring as a draw
As smelly as a drain is
Outside the kitchen door

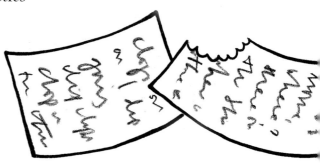

As hungry as a wave
That feeds upon the coast
As gaping as the grave
As GOTCHA! as a ghost

As fruitless as a cake of soap
As creeping-up as smoke
The reader of this poem, I hope,
Knows how to take a joke!

First Day at School

A millionbillionwillion miles from home
waiting for the bell to go. (To go where?)
Why are they all so big, other children?
So noisy? So much at home they
must have been born in uniform.
Lived all their lives in playgrounds.
Spent the years inventing games
that don't let me in. Games
that are rough, that swallow you up.

And the railings.
All around, the railings.
Are they to keep out wolves and monsters?
Things that carry off and eat children?
Things you don't take sweets from?
Perhaps they're to stop us getting out.
Running away from the lessins. Lessin.
What does a lessin look like?
Sounds small and slimy.
They keep them in glassrooms.
Whole rooms made out of glass. Imagine.

I wish I could remember my name.
Mummy said it would come in useful.
Like wellies. When there's puddles.
Yellowwellies. I wish she was here.
I think my name is sewn on somewhere.
Perhaps the teacher will read it for me.
Tea-cher. The one who makes the tea.

What I Love About School

What I love about school
    is the hurly-burly of the classroom,
    the sly humour of the teachers

What I hate about teachers
    is their reluctance to cartwheel
    down corridors

What I love about corridors
    is that the longer they are
    the louder the echo

What I hate about echo echo
    is its refusal to answer a straight
    question question

What I love about question
    is the proud admission
    of its own ignorance

What I hate about ignorance
    is the naive assumption
    that it is bliss

What I love about bliss
    is its willingness
    to rhyme with kiss

What I hate about kiss
    is the news of it going around
    like wildfire

What I love about wildfire
    is its dragon's breath
    and its hunger for life

What I hate about life
    is that as soon as you get the hang of it
    you run out of time

What I love about time
    is how it flies
    except when at school

What I hate about school
    is the hurly-burly of the playground,
    the sly humour of the teachers.

Head

The Head of our school
is called Mr Head.
Honestly, that's his name.

'My name is Head
and I'm the new Head,'
Is what he said when he came.

He's very, very nice
but it has to be said,
that our Head, Mr Head,
has a very large head.

It says 'Head' on his sports bag,
and 'Head' on the door,
but which of the heads
does the 'Head' stand for?

Class Warfare

I'm the most important
Person in the class

Twenty-four carat diamond
While all the rest are glass

Distinctions distinguish me
While others strive to pass

I'm en route for glory
While others are en masse

They're backdrops, they're bit parts
They're day-old candy floss

They provide the undercoat
For my enduring gloss

When I go down in history
I'll go down a storm

For I'm the most important
Person in the form

(If you don't believe me
Ask Daddy – he's the headmaster.)

Mums and Dads

My daddy's a lawyer
said Mort
He wears a wig when he goes to court

So does my mum
said Allister
And her wig's big cos she's a barrister

My dad drives a truck
said Gus
As wide as a playground as big as a bus

My mum's a chef
said Jocasta
She bakes her own bread and makes her own pasta

My daddy's a doctor
said Henrietta
He gives people pills to make them feel better

My mum's a model
said Rose
And she gets to keep all her beautiful clothes

My dad's a boxer
said Lee
So you'd better think twice before picking on me

My mum's a footballer
said Jane
And next week she's playing for England again

My dad's a runner
said Sid
Well that's what my mum said he did

My mum's a mum
said Sue
With three sons and five daughters what else
can she do?

My dad's a tattooist
said Liam
And Mum's got the crown jewels where no one can see 'em

My mum's a vicar
said Tessa
She works every day, even Sundays, God bless her

My dad's a detective
said Isabel
Though to look at him you couldn't tell

My mum's a dietitian
said Gaby
She shouts at ladies when they get flabby

My dad's unemployed
said Eliza
Though he used to be a careers adviser.

The Leader

I wanna be the leader
I wanna be the leader
Can I be the leader?
Can I? I can?
Promise? Promise?
Yippee, I'm the leader
I'm the leader

OK what shall we do?

The Boy with a Similar Name

When Raymond Gough joined our class
He was almost a year behind.
'Sanatorium,' said Mrs McBride
'So I want you all to be kind.'

'Roger, your names are similar
So let Raymond sit next to you
He'll need a friend to teach him the ropes
And show him what to do.'

Then teacher went back to teaching
And we went back to being taught
And I tried to be kind to Raymond
But it was harder than I thought.

For he was the colour of candlewax
And smelled of Dettol and Vick.
He was as thin as a sharpened pencil
And his glasses were milk-bottle thick.

Not only that but unfriendly
All muffled up in his shell.
Hobbies? Interests? Ambitions?
It was impossible to tell.

I was afraid of catching his yellowness
And smelling of second-hand Vick
And the only time I could be myself
Were the days when he was off sick.

But what proved to be contagious
Was his oddness, and I knew
That he was a victim ripe for bullying
And so by proxy, I was too.

'How's your brother, Raymond?'
The class began to tease,
'Do you share his dirty handkerchief?
Do you catch each other's fleas?'

'He's not my brother,' I shouted,
My cheeks all burning hot,
'He's a drippy four-eyed monster,
And he comes from the planet Snot.'

They laughed and I saw an opening
(Wouldn't you have done the same?)
I pointed a finger at Raymond
And joined in the bullying game.

He stopped coming to school soon after,
'Sanatorium,' said Mrs McBride.
He never came back and nobody knew
If he moved elsewhere or died.

I don't think of him very often
For when I do I blush with shame
At the thought of the pain I helped inflict
On the boy with a similar name.

It Wasn't Me, Miss

It wasn't me, Miss, it was 'er, Miss
Every lesson it's the same
I never do nothin'
But I always get the blame

I didn't smash that window
Or throw water on the floor
It wasn't me who put the frog
In Mrs Kelly's drawer

I didn't make rude noises
When yer back was turned
I was nowhere near the library
When the books got burned

It wasn't me, Miss, it was 'er, Miss
Would I tell fibs to you?
An' I didn't paint the hamster
That lovely powder blue

I didn't scratch the piano
It wasn't me who broke the chair
And any road, if I did
It wasn't me, it was 'er

She acts all sweet and innocent
But the minute that you're gone
She's Frankenstein and Reservoir Dogs
All rolled into one.

It wasn't me, Miss, it was 'er, Miss
… What? … Sit apart?
Don't be mean, Miss, we're a team, Miss
I'll be good, cross my heart!

Streemin

Im in the botom streme
Which meens Im not brigth
dont like reading
cant hardly rite

but all thesedivishns
arnt reely fair
look at the cemtery
no streemin there

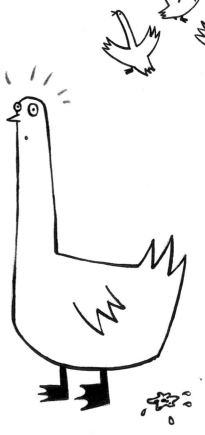

Harum Scarum

I am harum
I disturb the peace
I go around
saying boo to geese

I am harum scarum
a one man gang
diddle dum darum
bang bang bang

Butterfingers

When I was a child
I caught measles. Then
I caught mumps. After that
I caught tonsillitis. A month later
I caught influenza. As soon as I was better
I caught pneumonia. So my mother took me to see
The old wives
Who advised dipping my fingers
In butter every morning.
So I did. And since then
I haven't caught a thing.

Easy Money

Guess how old I am?
I bet you can't.
I bet you.
Go on guess.
Have a guess.

Wrong!
Have another.

Wrong!
Have another.

Wrong again!
Do you give in?

Seven years four months two weeks
five days three hours fifteen
minutes forty-eight seconds!
That's 20p you owe me.

Reward and Punishment

If you are very good I will give you:

A pillow of blue strawberries
A swimming pool of Häagen-Dasz
A mirror of imagination
A pocketful of yes's
A hiss of sleigh rides
A lunch box of swirling planets
A doorway of happy endings
A hedgerow of diamonds
A surfboard of dolphins
A cat's paw of tickles
A carton of fresh rainbow-juice
A forest of chocolate wardrobes

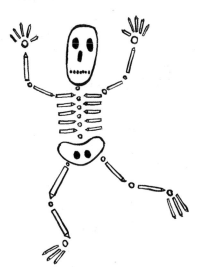

If you are naughty you will get:

A burst of balloon
A screech of wolf
A hoof of piggy bank
A twitch of sideways
A splinter of thirst
A precipice of banana skins
A tyrannosaurus of broccoli
A rucksack of bony elbows
A skeleton of lost pencils
A flag of inconvenience
A chill of false laughter
A blackboard of no way out

21

Plague Around

There's a plague around
There's a plague around
In every village
And every town

With big purple spots
And greenish ones too
There's a plague around
And it's waiting for you

There's a plague around
There's a plague around
Keep your eyes open
And don't make a sound

Or your ears will flap
And you'll start to cough
You'll sneeze and sneeze
Till your nose drops off

There's a plague around
There's a plague around
In every school
There's a playground

You'll burst out laughing
And run around
When you get into
The playground

There's a playground
There's a playground
In every school
There's a playground.

Riddle

I'm older than my eldest son
But younger than my mother
One hand has 'left' tattooed on
'Right' is on the other.
What am I?

Answer:
silly

23

The Magic Pebble

My favourite thing is a pebble
That I found on a beach in Wales
It looks like any other
But its magic never fails

It does my homework for me
Makes difficult sums seem clear
School dinners taste delicious
It makes teachers disappear

It turns water into lemonade
A bully into a frog
When I'm in need of company
It becomes a friendly dog

Close your eyes, make a wish
And you're in a foreign land
Space travel is so easy
Simply hold it in your hand

My favourite thing is a pebble
It means all the world to me
I couldn't bear to be without it
(… But it's yours for 20p)

My Brilliant Friend

He's brilliant at karate
He's brilliant at darts
He's brilliant at acting
He gets all the best parts

He's brilliant at swimming
He's brilliant at skates
He's brilliant at juggling
With real china plates

He's brilliant at poetry
He's brilliant at rhyme
He's brilliant at lessons
He comes top every time

He's Brilliant just Brilliant
With a capital B
(Although he's only average
In comparison with me).

A Good Poem

I like a good poem,
one with lots of fighting
in it. Blood, and the
clanging of armour. Poems

against Scotland are good,
and poems that defeat
the French with crossbows.
I don't like poems that

aren't about anything.
Sonnets are wet and
a waste of time.
Also poems that don't

know how to rhyme.
If I was a poem
I'd play football and
get picked for England.

A Great Poem

This poem is great.
Wondrous and fabulous
it can hardly wait

to get out there
among you all
and give it to you straight.

If it were a painting
they would hang it
in the Tate.

It's lyrical
It's musical
Intellectually first-rate.

Five-Six-Seven-Eight
What do we appreciate?
This poem.

(Who says it's great?)

Roger McGough

Apostrophe

'twould be nice to be
an apostrophe
floating
above an s
hovering
like a paper kite
in between the its
eavesdropping, tiptoeing
high above the thats
an inky comet
spiralling
the highest tossed
of hats

Watchwords

watch the words

watch words

the watchword

is watch

words are

sly as boots

takeyoureyesoffthemforaminute

and they're up and away all over the place

Smithereens

I spend my days
collecting smithereens.
I find them on buses
in department stores
and on busy pavements.

At restaurant tables
I pick up the leftovers
of polite conversation
At railway stations
the tearful debris
of parting lovers.

I pocket my eavesdroppings
and store them away.
I make things out of them.
Nice things, sometimes.
Sometimes odd, like this.

The Power of Poets

The man on the pavement
outside, giving change
to the old tramp and
feeling good isn't me.
I am the pavement.
I could have been
the tramp or even
the change. However
I choose to be the
pavement and it is
my poem. Such is
the power of poets.

A Poem Just For Me

Where am I now when I need me
Suddenly where have I gone
I'm so alone here without me
Tell me please what have I done?

Once I did most things together
I went for walks hand in hand
I shared my life so completely
I met my every demand.

Tell me I'll come back tomorrow
I'll keep my arms open wide
Tell me that I'll never leave me
My place is here at my side.

Maybe I've simply mislaid me
Like an umbrella or key
So until the day that I come my way
Here is a poem just for me.

The Super-Word Market

(A poem for forty-two words)

I want to write a new poem.
What words shall I choose?
I go in. The variety is endless.
Images stretch into infinity.

I dither. Can't make up my mind.
Inspiration becomes impatient.
Stamps its feet. Panicking
I grab the nearest forty-two

Choose the Rhyme

The sun's too hot and the moon's too cold
The clouds are too young and the stars too old
The Queen's too kind and the King's too grumpy
The pillow's too soft and the bed's too lumpy
The pig's too bare and the lamb's too fleecy
The stew's too thin and the soup's too greasy
The sea's too wet and the beach is too stony
The poem's too long and the poet's too …

moany? groany? bony? macaroni? Al Capone?

Waxing Lyrical

I polish the dining room table
Bring a shine to the bentwood chairs
You can see your face in the wardrobe
Mind you don't slip on the stairs

I polish the eggs in the kitchen
The bread before I toast it
Cover the chicken with elbow grease
And rub before I roast it

I polish my grandfather's trousers
(At the knees, where he likes them to shine)
My grandmother's nose, how it sparkles!
And her dentures, aren't they divine?

I polish the flowers in the garden
The front of the house, brick by brick
If the clouds would stand still for a minute
I'd wipe the dust off right quick

I polish the car every Sunday
I polish the Sunday as well
I polish the years, and the yearnings
I polish the fears and the smell

I polish the reasons for living
I polish the truth and the lies
I polish your innermost secrets
I polish the earth and the skies.

I polish the language of angels
The horn of the unicorn too
If you think this poem is rubbish
Then I'll call round and polish off you!

I Wish I Were a Crochet

I wish I were a crochet
I'd sing and dance and play
among the dotted minims
all the livelong day

I'd swing from stave to stave
up and down I'd climb
Then crawl from bar to bar
singing all the time

I wish I were a crochet
or a semibreve
I'd find a lady quaver
and her I'd never leave

We'd run around the manuscript
a pair of little ravers
Get married pianissimo
and raise lots of semi-quavers

The All-Purpose Children's Poem

The first verse contains a princess
    Two witches (one evil, one good)
There is a castle in it somewhere
    And a dark and tangled wood.

The second has ghosts and vampires
    Monsters with foul-smelling breath
It sends shivers down the book spine
    And scares everybody to death.

The third is one of my favourites
    With rabbits in skirts and trousers
Who talk to each other like we do
    And live in neat little houses.

The fourth verse is bang up to date
    And in it anything goes.
Set in the city, it doesn't rhyme
    (Although, in a way it does.)

The fifth is set in the future
    (And as you can see, it's the last)
When the Word was made Computer
    And books are a thing of the past.

The Cackle

Cut the cackle
and get the gist

heat the kettle
and wet the wrist

raise the hackle
and cock the snook

shake the rattle
and sling the hook

trim the tackle
and nook the cranny

lick the pickle
and tickle your granny.

No Grannies in This Poem

There are no grannies in this poem
I wouldn't let one in if she tried
It's no way to treat old ladies, I know
But I've kept them waiting outside

It's not raining there at the moment
And we are in for a settled spell
They've got lots of things to chatter about
And they get on reasonably well

This poem, you see, is about witches
And subjects that grannies don't care for
Like vampires and aliens from outer space
Waging intergalactic warfare

So if you want a poem about grannies
I suggest you go look elsewhere
For there are no grannies in this poem.
Definitely not, definitely not.

Pillow Talk

Last night I heard my pillow talk
What amazing things it said
About the fun that pillows have
Before it's time for bed

The bedroom is their playground
A magical place to be
(Not a room for peace and quiet
Like it is for you and me)

They divebomb off the wardrobe
Do backflips off the chair
Use the mattress as a trampoline
Turn somersaults in the air

It's Leapfrog then Pass the Slipper
Handstands and cartwheels all round
Wrestling and swinging on curtains
And all with hardly a sound

But by and by the feathers fly
And they get out of puff
So with scarves and ties they bind their eyes
For a game of Blind Man's Buff

They tiptoe out on the landing
Although it's a dangerous place
(If granny met one on the stairs
Imagine the look on her face!)

It's pillows who open cupboard drawers
To mess and rummage about
(And you end up by getting blamed
For something they left out)

I'd quite fancy being a pillow
Playing games and lying in bed
If I didn't have to spend each night
Under your big snoring head!

I've Taken to My Bed

I've taken to my bed
(And my bed has taken to me)
We're getting married in the spring
How happy we shall be

We'll raise lots of little bunks
A sleeping-bag or two
Take my advice, find a bed that's nice
Lie down and say: 'I love you.'

Wink

I took 40 winks
yesterday afternoon
and another 40 today.
In fact I get through
about 280 winks a week.
Which is about 14,560
winks a year.
(The way I'm going on
I'll end up looking like a wink.)

Top

Dad, risen and dizzy
from sleep, would say,
'I slept like a top.'

This puzzled me.
Top of what?
Top of the milk?
Top of the class?
Top of the wardrobe?
Top of the morning?

So I asked him.
'Spinning top,' he said.

Funny, I thought,
to spend all night
spinning round the bedroom.
No wonder he looked so tired every morning!

The Missing Sock

I found my sock
beneath the bed.
'Where have you been
all week?' I said.

'Hiding away,'
the sock replied.
'Another day on your foot
and I would have died!'

I've Got a Cold

I've got a cold
And it's not funny

My throat is numb
My nose is runny

My ears are burning
My fingers are itching

My teeth are wobbly
My eyebrows are twitching

My kneecaps have slipped
My bottom's like jelly

The button's come off
My silly old belly

My chin has doubled
My toes are twisted

My ankles have swollen
My elbows are blistered

My back is all spotty
My hair's turning white

I sneeze through the day
And cough through the night

I've got a cold
And I'm going insane

(Apart from all that
I'm as right as rain.)

Wouldn't It Be Funny If You Didn't Have a Nose?

You couldn't smell your dinner
If you didn't have a nose
You couldn't tell a dirty nappy
From a summer rose
You couldn't smell the ocean
Or the traffic, I suppose
Oh wouldn't it be funny
If you didn't have a nose?

You couldn't smell your mummy
If you didn't have a nose
You couldn't tell an orange
From a row of smelly toes
You couldn't smell the burning
(Think how quick a fire grows)
Wouldn't it be funny
If you didn't have a nose?

Where would we be without our hooters?
Nothing else would really suit us.
What would we sniff through?
How would we sneeze?
What would we wipe
Upon our sleeves?

You couldn't smell a rat
If you didn't have a nose
You couldn't tell a duchess
From a herd of buffaloes
And . . . mmmm that Gorgonzola
As it starts to decompose
Oh wouldn't it be funny
If you didn't have a nose?

Where would we be without our hooters?
Nothing else would really suit us.
And think of those who
Rub their noses
Life would be tough for
Eskimoses

You couldn't wear your glasses
If you didn't have a nose
And what would bullies aim for
When it came to blows?
Where would nostrils be without them?
When it's runny how it glows
Oh wouldn't it be funny
If you didn't have a . . .

        have a . . .

        have a . . .

            a . . .

            a . . . choo!

Hide and Seek

When I played as a kid
How I longed to be caught
But whenever I hid
Nobody sought.

Itch

My sister had an itch
    I asked if it was catching.
'Catch,' she said, and threw it.
    Now I'm the one who's scratching.

Tantrums

When my sister starts to frown
I'm always on my guard

Yesterday she threw a tantrum
But it missed me by a yard.

Bottom

Who'd be a bottom? Not me.

Always facing the wrong way.
To go for a walk
And not be able to see
Where you are going.

To be sat upon all day.
Smacked. Called rude names.
Whistled at. Laughed at.
The butt of a hundred jokes.

Faithful to the end.
An undercover agent
Working all hours
And getting no thanks for it.

Alas, poor bottom.

Sky in the Pie!

Waiter, there's a sky in my pie
Remove it at once if you please
You can keep your incredible sunsets
I ordered mincemeat and cheese

I can't stand nightingales singing
Or clouds all burnished with gold
The whispering breeze is disturbing the peas
And making my chips go all cold

I don't care if the chef is an artist
Whose canvases hang in the Tate
I want two veg. and puff pastry
Not the Universe heaped on my plate

OK I'll try just a spoonful
I suppose I've got nothing to lose
Mm ... the colours quite tickle the palette
With a blend of delicate hues

The sun has a custardy flavour
And the clouds are as light as air
And the wind a chewier texture
(With a hint of cinammon there?)

This sky is simply delicious
Why haven't I tried it before?
I can chew my way through to Eternity
And still have room left for more

Having acquired a taste for the Cosmos
I'll polish this sunset off soon
I can't wait to tuck into the night sky
Waiter! Please bring me the Moon!

The Burp

One evening at supper
A little girl burped.
'Tut, tut,' said mother.
'What do you say?' said father.

Her brother giggled.
'It's not funny,' said father.
'Pardon,' said the little girl.
'That's better,' said mother.

And all was quickly forgotten.
Except, that is, by the burp.
It had only just been born
And already everybody was apologizing.

What sort of person gives birth
And then says 'pardon'?
What sort of relative giggles
Then looks away, embarrassed?

Hurt, the baby burp hovered near the ceiling
Looked down at the one who had brought it up
Then escaped through an open window,
Never to return.

Lollidollops

I like a nice
dollop of ice cream
on my porridge

I like a nice
dollop of ice cream
in my tea

But the dollop
I like the most
is the one
I have on toast

With my eggs, bacon,
mushrooms, beans, sausages,
spaghetti, black puddings, pancakes,
apple pie, mushy peas, tomatoes, kidneys and custard.

Bun Fight

The buns are having a fight
There are currants on the floor
The custards egg them on
'More,' they chorus, 'more.'

The doughnuts form a ring
'Ding, ding!' and the seconds are out
An eccles cake is taking bets
As to who will win the bout.

The referee is a muffin
The timekeeper is a scone
There are five rounds still to go
And the custards egg them on.

The chelsea bun is tiring
And hoping for a draw
When the bath bun throws an upper-cut
That brings him to the floor.

The muffin slowly counts him out
And the bath bun's arm is raised
While through the window, passers-by
Look into the cake-shop, amazed.

No Peas For the Wicked

No peas for the wicked
No carrots for the damned
No parsnips for the naughty
  O Lord we pray

No sprouts for the shameless
No cabbage for the shady
No lettuce for the lecherous
  No way, no way

No potatoes for the deviants
No radish for the riff-raff
No spinach for the spineless
  Lock them away

No beetroot for the boasters
No mange tout for the mobsters
No corn-on-the-cob et cetera
  (Shall we call it a day?)

Keep Your Eyes Peeled

In my field of vision
In that watery field
Grow potatoes with eyes in
Which is why I keep them peeled.

Cabbage

The cabbage is a funny veg.
All crisp, and green, and brainy.
I sometimes wear one on my head
When it's cold and rainy.

Vegetarians

Vegetarians are cruel, unthinking people.
Everybody knows that a carrot screams when grated.
That a peach bleeds when torn apart.
Do you believe an orange insensitive
to thumbs gouging out its flesh?
That tomatoes spill their brains painlessly?
Potatoes, skinned alive and boiled,
the soil's little lobsters.
Don't tell me it doesn't hurt
when peas are squeezed from the pod,
the hide flayed off sprouts,
cabbage shredded, onions beheaded.

Throw in the trowel
and lay down the hoe.
Mow no more
Let my people go!

'US Flies in Hamburgers'

*Newspaper headline referring to hamburgers being
airlifted to feed homesick US marines.*

If you go down the High Street today
You'll be sure of a big surprise
When you order your favourite burger
With a milkshake and regular fries.

For the secret is out I tell you no lies
They've stopped using beef in favour of flies.

Flies, flies, big juicy flies,
Flies as American as apple pies.

Horseflies, from Texas, as big as your thumb
Are sautéed with onions and served in a bun.

Free-range bluebottles, carefully rinsed
Are smothered in garlic, and painlessly minced.

Black-eyed bees with stings intact
Add a zesty zing, and that's a fact.

Colorado beetles, ants from Kentucky,
Rhode Island roaches, and if you're unlucky

Baltimore bedbugs (and even horrider)
Leeches as squashy as peaches from Florida.

Flies, flies, big juicy flies,
Flies as American as Mom's apple pies.

It's lovely down in MacDingles today
But if you don't fancy flies
Better I'd say to keep well away
Stay home and eat Birds' Eyes.

A Weak Poem

(To be read lying down)

Oh dear, this poem is very weak
It can hardly stand up straight
Which comes from eating junk food
And going to bed too late.

The Fight of the Year

'And there goes the bell for the third month
and Winter comes out of its corner looking groggy
Spring leads with a left to the head
followed by a sharp right to the body
  daffodils
  primroses
  crocuses
  snowdrops
  lilacs
  violets
  pussy willow
Winter can't take much more punishment
and Spring shows no signs of tiring
  tadpoles
  squirrels
  baa-lambs
  badgers
  bunny rabbits
  mad march hares
  horses and hounds
Spring is merciless
Winter won't go the full twelve rounds

bobtail clouds
scallywaggy winds
the sun
a pavement artist
in every town
A left to the chin
and Winter's down!
tomatoes
radish
cucumber
onions
beetroot
celery
and any
amount
of lettuce
for dinner
Winter's out for the count
Spring is the winner!'

61

Autumn Poem

litter
    is
        turning
           brown
             and
               the
                 road
                   above
                 is
              filled
            with
         hitch
       hikers
     heading
  south

First Haiku of Spring

cuck oo cuck oo cuck
oo cuck oo cuck oo cuck oo
cuck oo cuck oo cuck

Trees Are Great

Trees are great, they just stand and wait
They don't cry when they're teased
They don't eat much and they seldom shout
Trees are easily pleased

Trees are great, they like to congregate
For meetings in the park
They dance and sway, they stay all day
And talk till well after dark

Trees are great, they accept their fate
When it's pouring down with rain
They don't wear macs, it runs off their backs
But you never hear them complain

So answer me, please, if there weren't any trees
Where would naughty boys climb?
Where would lovers carve their names?
Where would little birds nest?
Where would we hang the leaves?

Why Trees Have Got It All Wrong

Trees have got it all wrong
because they shed their leaves
as soon as it gets cold.

If they had any sense
they'd take them off in June
and let the scented breezes

whiffle through the branches
cooling the bare torso.
In high summer, more so.

☆   ☆   ☆

Come autumn (not the fall)
they'd put on a new coat:
thick leaves, waxed and fur-lined

to keep them warm as toast,
whatever the weather.
Trees, get it together!

* Storm

They're at it again
the wind and the rain
It all started
when the wind
took the window
by the collar
and shook it
with all its might
Then the rain
butted in
What a din
they'll be at it all night
Serves them right
if they go home in the morning
and the sky won't let them in

The Snowman

Mother, while you were at the shops
and I was snoozing in my chair
I heard a tap at the window
saw a snowman standing there

He looked so cold and miserable
I almost could have cried
so I put the kettle on
and invited him inside

I made him a cup of cocoa
to warm the cockles of his nose
then he snuggled in front of the fire
for a cosy little doze

He lay there warm and smiling
softly counting sheep
I eavesdropped for a little while
then I too fell asleep

Seems he woke and tiptoed out
exactly when I'm not too sure
it's a wonder you didn't see him
as you came in through the door

(oh, and by the way,
the kitten's made a puddle on the floor)

Haiku

Snowman in a field
listening to the raindrops
wishing him farewell

Snow and Ice Poems

(i)   Our street is dead lazy
        especially in winter.
        Some mornings you wake up
        and it's still lying there
        saying nothing. Huddled
        under its white counterpane.

        But soon the lorries arrive
        like angry mums,
        pull back the blankets
        and send it shivering
        off to work.

(ii)   To
        boggan?
        or not
        to boggan?
        That is the question.

(iii)   Winter
morning.
Snowflakes
for breakfast.
The street
outside
quiet
as a
long
white
bandage.

(iv)   The time I like best
is 6 a.m.
and the snow is six inches deep

Which I'm yet to discover
cos I'm under the cover
and fast, fast asleep.

The Midnight Skaters

It is midnight in the ice rink
   And all is cool and still.
Darkness seems to hold its breath
   Nothing moves, until

Out of the kitchen, one by one,
   The cutlery comes creeping,
Quiet as mice to the brink of the ice
   While all the world is sleeping.

Then suddenly, a serving-spoon
   Switches on the light,
And the silver swoops upon the ice
   Screaming with delight.

The knives are high-speed skaters
   Round and round they race,
Blades hissing, sissing,
   Whizzing at a dizzy pace.

Forks twirl like dancers
   Pirouetting on the spot.
Teaspoons (who take no chances)
   Hold hands and giggle a lot.

All night long the fun goes on
    Until the sun, their friend,
Gives the warning signal
    That all good things must end.

So they slink back to the darkness
    Of the kitchen cutlery-drawer
And steel themselves to wait
    Until it's time to skate once more.

At eight the canteen ladies
    Breeze in as good as gold
To lay the tables and wonder
    Why the cutlery is so cold.

In Good Hands

Wherever night falls

The earth is always

There to catch it.

Downhill Racer

Down

the

snow

white

page

we

slide.

From

side

to

side

we

glide.

Pass

obstacles

with

ease.

Words

on

skis.

Look out.

Here

comes

a

poem

in

a

hurry!

Uphill Climb

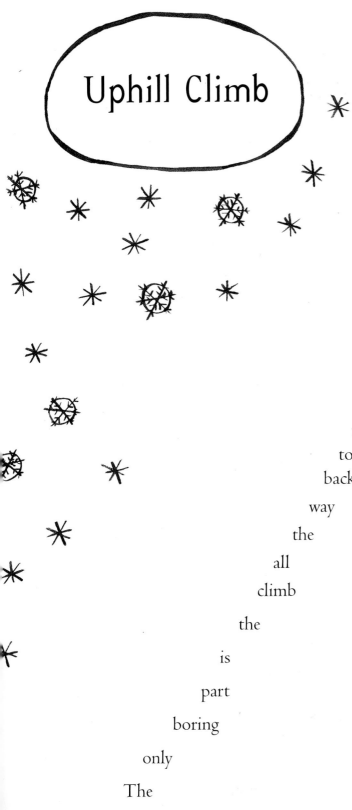

Wheeeeee

Three
Two
One
go.
another
have
to
top
the
to
back
way
the
all
climb
the
is
part
boring
only
The

Pinning up a Notice

the sun
hasn't got me fooled
not for a minute
just when
you're beginning to believe
that   grass is green
and   skies are blue
and   colour is king
hey   ding a ding ding
and
a
   host
         of
             other
                  golden
                       et ceteras
before you know where you are
he's slunk off somewhere
and pinned up a notice saying:

MOON

Mrs Moon

Mrs Moon
sitting up in the sky
little old lady
rock-a-bye
with a ball of fading light
and silvery needles
knitting the night

Icy Fingers

Despite the cold
A line of old trees
Playing with the moon

Tossing it
From one to the other
Never missing a catch.

The Sad Astronomer

His telescope is beyond repair.
Tonight he opens the sky
but cannot read it.
The stars, a jumble,
dance before his eyes.

Mad Ad

An advertising whizz-kid
thought it a disgrace
That no one had exploited
the possibilities in space
Discussed it with a client
who agreed and very soon
A thousand miles of neon tubing
were transported to the moon.

Now no one can ignore it
the product's selling fine
The night they turned the moon
into a Coca-Cola sign.

One More Battle

Who's that sailor
stern and solemn?
'Tis Lord Nelson
down from his column.

Why goes he limping
up the street?
In search of a long-lost
English Fleet.

Why driven now
to such despair?
The need to breathe
some clean fresh air.

Give and Take

I give you clean air
You give me poisonous gas.
I give you mountains
You give me quarries.

I give you pure snow
You give me acid rain.
I give you spring fountains
You give me toxic canals.

I give you a butterfly
You gave me a plastic bottle.
I give you a blackbird
You gave me a stealth bomber.

I give you abundance
You give me waste.
I give you one last chance
You give me excuse after excuse.

Five-Car Family

We're a five-car family
We got what it takes
Eight thousand cc
Three different makes

One each for the kids
I run two
One for the missus
When there's shopping to do

Cars are Japanese of course
Subaru and Mazda
And the Nissan that the missus takes
Nippin' down to Asda

We're a load of noisy parkers
We never do it neat
Drive the neighbours crazy
When we take up half the street

Unleaded petrol?
That's gotta be a joke
Stepping on the gas we like
The smoke to make you choke

Carbon monoxide
Take a deep breath
Benzine dioxide
Automanic death

Cos it's all about noise
And it's all about speed
And it's all about power
And it's all about greed

And it's all about fantasy
And it's all about dash
And it's all about machismo
And it's all about cash

And it's all about blood
And it's all about gore
And it's all about oil
And it's all about war

And it's all about money
And it's all about spend
And it's all about time
That it came to an end.

Everything Touches

Everything touches, life interweaves
Starlight and wood smoke, ashes and leaves
Birdsong and thunder, acid and rain
Everything touches, unbroken chain

Rainstorm and rainbow, warrior and priest
Stingray and dolphin, beauty and beast
Heartbeat and high tide, ebb tide and flow
The universe in a crystal of snow

Snowdrop and deathcap, hangman and clown
Walls that divide come tumbling down
Seen through the night, the glimmer of day
Light is but darkness worn away

Blackness and whiteness, sunset and dawn
Those gone before, those yet to be born
Past and future, distance and time
Atom to atom, water to wine

Look all around and what do you see?
Everything touches, you're touching me
Look all around and what do you see?
Everything touches, you're touching me.

Borrowed Time

Apparently we are all living
On Borrowed Time.
What I want to know is
Who borrowed it, and from whom?

And another thing . . .
If we give it back
Can we borrow another?

Eye Sore

I saw
a building
soar
into the sky

making
the sky's
eye
sore.

Estate

Mother!
They're building a town centre in the bedroom
A car park in the lounge, it's a sin.

There's a block of flats going up in the toilet
What a shocking estate we are in.

Neighbourhood Watch

It's a sin
It's a crime
Now we can't tell the time
Our neighbourhood watch
Has been stolen!

Fire Guard

My wife bought a fire guard for the living room
Seems a nice sort of chap.

Zebra Crossing

There is a Lollipopman
At the zebra crossing
With lollipops
He is trying
To lure zebras across
He makes me cross.
I cross.

I Say I Say I Say

I say I say I say
A funny thing happened on my way here today
The buildings had hiccups, the road ran away
Buses grew hair in the silliest places
Traffic lights chuckled and pulled funny faces
Three-legged lamp posts chased little dogs
The moon was mugged by stars wearing clogs
Policemen and policewomen danced on the beat
A zebra crossing galloped off down the street
Beggars gave money to passers-by
There was an old lady who swallowed a …?
The town's in a tizzy, it's gone off its head
It's making me dizzy, I'm going back to bed.

A Cat, a Horse and the Sun

a cat mistrusts the sun
keeps out of its way
only where sun and shadow meet
it moves

a horse loves the sun
it basks all day
snorts
and beats its hooves

the sun likes horses
but hates cats
that is why it makes hay
and heats tin roofs

Pussy Pussy Puddle Cat

Pussy pussy puddle cat
what do you think
you're playing at
making puddles
on the mat
chairs and tables
don't do that!

Marmalade

A ginger tom
name of Marmalade
shaved his whiskers
with a razor blade

Last mistake
he ever made.

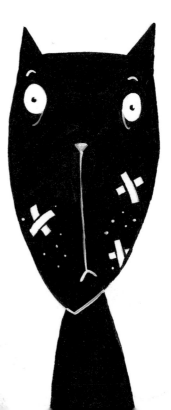

The Cats' Protection League

Midnight. A knock at the door.
Open it? Better had.
Three heavy cats, mean and bad.

They offer protection. I ask, 'What for?'
The Boss-cat snarls, 'You know the score.
Listen man and listen good

If you wanna stay in the neighbourhood,
Pay your dues or the toms will call
And wail each night on the backyard wall.

Mangle the flowers, and as for the lawn
A smelly minefield awaits you at dawn.'
These guys meant business without a doubt

Three cans of tuna, I handed them out.
They then disappeared like bats into hell
Those bad, bad cats from the CPL.

Mafia Cats

We're the Mafia cats
    Bugsy, Franco and Toni
We're crazy for pizza
    With hot pepperoni

We run all the rackets
    From gambling to vice
On St Valentine's Day
    We massacre mice

We always wear shades
    To show that we're meanies
Big hats and sharp suits
    And drive Lamborghinis

We're the Mafia cats
    Bugsy, Franco and Toni
Love Sicilian wine
    And cheese macaroni

But we have a secret
    (And if you dare tell
You'll end up with the kitten
    At the bottom of the well

Or covered in concrete
  And thrown into the deep
For this is one secret
  You really must keep.)

We're the Cosa Nostra
  Run the scams and the fiddles
But at home we are
  Mopsy, Ginger and Tiddles.

Cousin Reggie

Cousin Reggie
who adores the sea
lives in the Midlands
unfortunately.

He surfs down escalators
in department stores
and swims in the High Street
on all of his fours.

Sunbathes on the pavement
paddles in the gutter
(I think our Reggie's
a bit of a nutter).

Cousin Nell

Cousin Nell
married a frogman
in the hope
that one day
he would turn into a
handsome prince.

Instead he turned into
a sewage pipe
near Gravesend
and was never seen again.

Uncle Terry

Uncle Terry was a skydiver.
He liked best
the earth spread out beneath him
like a spring-cleaned counterpane.
The wind his safety net.

He free fell every day
and liked it so much
he decided to stay.
And they say he's still there
sunbathing in the air.

He sleeps each night
tucked up in moonlight
wakes at dawn
and chases clouds.

Living off the food birds bring
Uncle Terry on the wing
Away from it all
Dizzy with joy.

Eno

To be a sumo wrestler
 It pays to be fat.
'Nonsense,' said Eno,
 'I don't believe that.'

So he took his skinny
 little frame
to Tokyo
 in search of fame.

But even with God on
 his side
Eno got trod on
 and died.

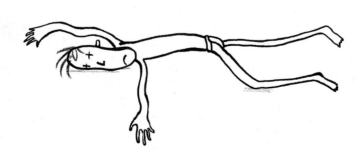

All's Well That Ends

Peter was awake as soon as daylight sidled into his
bedroom. Saturday at last. He jumped out of bed and
flung open the curtains. Thank goodness, he thought,
not a cloud in the sky. As he gazed out of the window, he
wondered about the day ahead. Would his school team
win the county cricket trophy? (*No.*) Would he score his
first century? (*No, lbw second ball.*) Would
Helen be at the party in the evening? (*Yes.*) Would she
let him dance with her, walk her home and kiss her? (*No,
she'd spend all night smooching and snogging with O'Leary.*)
Would the police discover Grandma's body
behind the woodshed? (*Yes, on Monday.*) And if so,
would they think it was an accident? (*No, sorry.*) Or
suicide? (*Hardly.*) Would he be incarcerated? (*What's
that?*) Put in prison (*Yes.*)

But during his time inside, wouldn't he determine to
make amends, study hard and gain early parole?
Wouldn't he find a steady job and settle down? One day
meet a decent girl and raise a family? Eventually,
wouldn't he own a national chain of DIY supermarkets,
give money to charity, become a model citizen respected
and loved by the whole community?
Say yes (*No.*)
But surely all's well that ends? (*Well . . . . . .*

Cautionary Tale

A little girl called Josephine
Was fair of face and reasonably clean
But at school she wore a dunce's cap
And her father, taking out a map

Said: 'She'll learn more if she comes with me
About the world and life at sea.
What she needs is a trip on my schooner
I'm surprised I didn't think of it sooner.

For I'm captain of the *Hesperus*
And I think I know what's best for us.'
And thereupon a most dreadful fate
Befell her, which I'll now relate.

It was winter when they left the port
(in retrospect they shouldn't ought)
Setting sail for the Spanish Main
Despite warnings of a hurricane.

Three days out there came the gale
Even the skipper he turned pale
And as for little Josephine
She turned seven shades of green

As the schooner rocked from port to starboard
Across the decks poor Josie scarpered
She ran from the fo'c'sle to the stern
(Some folks'll never learn)

Crying: 'Stop the boat, I want to go home.'
But unheeding, the angry foam
Swamped the decks. Her dad did curse
Knowing things would go from bad to worse

He called his daughter to his side
'Put on my seaman's coat,' he cried
'You'll be safe 'til the storm has passed.'
Then bound her tightly to the mast.

And pass it did, but sad to say
Not for a fortnight and a day.
By then the ship had foundered
And all the crew had drownded.

And reported later in the press
Was a story that caused much distress
Of a couple walking on the shore
And of the dreadful sight they saw

Tied to a mast, a few bones picked clean
All that remained of poor Josephine.

MORAL
Stay on at school, get your GCSEs
Let others sail the seven seas.

Moany Margaret

Moany Margaret
Day and night
One's too dark
One's too bright

    Moany Margaret
    Bread and honey
    One's too chewy
    One's too runny

Moany Margaret
Cello and flute
One's too stringy
One's too cute

    Moany Margaret
    Sea and sand
    One's too wet
    One's too bland

Moany Margaret
Cat and pony
One's too furry
One's too bony

grumble

groan

lament

wail

complain

Moany Margaret
Nat and Matty
One's too fat
One's too chatty

Moany Margaret
Mum and dad
One is gone
One is sad

Moany Margaret
So they name her
Margaret moans
Who can blame her?

sigh

carp whine

gripe grouse

whinge moan

fuss

Bucket

every evening after tea
grandad would take his bucket for a walk

An empty bucket

When i asked him why
he said because it was easier to carry
than a full one

grandad had
an answer
for everything

Strangeways

Granny's canary
Escaped from its cage
It's up on the roof
In a terrible rage

Hurling abuse
And making demands
That granny fails
To understand

'Lack of privacy'
'Boring old food'
It holds up placards
Painted and rude

It's not coming down
The canary warns
Till gran carries out
Major reforms

The message has spread
And now for days
Cage-birds have been acting
In very strange ways.

Blue Macaw

I used to keep
   a blue macaw
in my bedside
   bottom drawer

But he was never
   happy there
among my socks
   and underwear

He pined for sunshine
   trees galore
as in Brazil
   and Ecuador

Knowing then
   what I must do
I journeyed south
   as far as Kew

In the Gardens
   set him free
(wasn't that macaw-
   ful of me?)

Wiwis

To amuse
    emus
on warm summer nights

    Kiwis
do wiwis
from spectacular heights.

Ostrich

One morning
an ostrich
buried his head
in the sand
and fell asleep

On waking
he couldn't remember
where he'd buried it.

Crow

A crow is a crow is a crow
In the bird popularity poll
We are the lowest of the low
But do we care? No.

While others twitter on and on, or worse
Bang out the same three notes
Of musical Morse, we refrain.
If there's 'owt to caw, we caw.

Long since banned from the dawn chorus
We lie in bed until lunchtime
Then leisurely flap down
And bag a few smug worms.

Potter about in the afternoon
Call on friends, or simply bide.
For the night that others hide from
Is the time that we like best.

Nestled in treetops gently swaying
We stretch out to the sky
And hold court with the moon.
Stargazers we. The thinkers.

Looking deep into the heavens
We drift and drift and drift
Up and up into the blue black
Into the very crowness of the universe.

A crow is a crow is a crow
In the bird popularity poll
We are the lowest of the low
But do we care? No.

Seagulls

Seagulls are eagles
with no head for heights

For soggy old crusts
they get into fights

Out-of-tune buskers
beggars and screechers

Seagulls are not
my favourite creatures.

Love a Duck

I love a duck called Jack
He's my very favourite pet
But last week he took poorly
So I took him to the vet.

The vet said: 'Lad, the news is bad,
Your duck has lost its quack
And there's nowt veterinary science
Can do to bring it back.'

A quackless duck? What thankless luck!
Struck dumb without a word
Rendered mute like a bunged-up flute
My splendid, tongue-tied bird.

All day now on the duvet
He sits and occasionally sighs
Dreaming up a miracle
A faraway look in his eyes.

Like an orphan for his mother
Like a maiden for her lover
Waiting silently is Jack
For the gab to come back

For the gift of tongues that goes . . .

Why Do Sheep

Why do sheep
have curly coats?

To keep the wind
out of their froats

A Domesticated Donkey

A domesticated donkey from Slough
Wished to knit a new jumper but how?
  Attempts with her ears
  Resulted in tears
So instead, she knitted her brow.

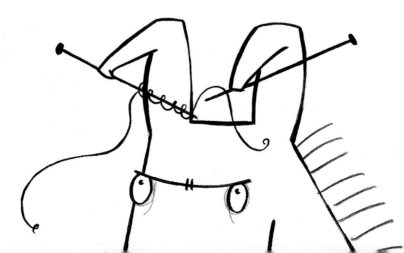

Poor Old Dead Horses

Don't give your rocking horse
To the old rag and bony

He'll go straight to the knacker
And haggle for money

The stirrups are torn off
The bridle and harness

Chopped up for firewood
It is thrown on the furnace

And the water that boils
Is chucked down the sluices

To wash away what remains
Of poor old dead horses.

Hundreds and Thousands

The sound of hounds
on red sand thundering

Hundreds and thousands
of mouths glistening

The blood quickening
Thunder and lightning

The hunted in dread
of the hundreds running

The sound of thunder
A white moon reddening

Thousands of mad hounds
on red sand marauding

Thundering onwards
in hundreds and thundreds

Thundreds and thundreds
Thundering   Thundering

Said the Water Boatman

Said the Water Boatman
  To the Water Boatmaid
'Won't you marry me?
  We'll leave this boring pond behind
And sail across the sea.'

  Said the Water Boatmaid
To the Water Boatman
  'Thanks, but I've no wish
To leave my natural habitat
  And feed the deep-sea fish.'

So the Water Boatman
  Set off the next day
To cross the ocean wide
  Some say he lives on a tropical isle
Others say he died.

  Said the Water Boatmaid
'How good to be free
  And frail and pretty and young.'
And she sang a wee song
  As she drifted along.

And she didn't hear the snap
Of the dragonfly's tongue.

And she didn't hear the snap
Of the dragonfly's tongue.

A Porcupine

A porcupine
   that lost its quills
ran away from home
   and took to the hills

All day long
   it cried as it crawled
'No one can love
   a creature so bald.'

But it was wrong.

A handsome kestrel
   dropped by to say
'I Love You! I Love You!'
   Then snatched it away.

Pull the Other One

A crab, I am told,
 will not bite
or poison you
 just for spite.

Won't lie in wait
 beneath a stone
until one morning,
 out alone

You poke a finger
 like a fool
into an innocent-
 looking pool.

Won't leap out
 and grab your hand
drag you sideways
 o'er the sand

To the bottom
 of the sea
And eat you, dressed,
 for Sunday tea.

A crab, I am told,
   is a bundle of fun
(With claws like that
   Pull the other one.)

Goldfish

Goldfish
are not
boldfish

They cry
when they
fall over

They tittletat
and chew
the fat

And are glad
when it's
all over.

115

Didgeridoo

Catfish
take catnaps on seabeds
Sticklebacks
stick like glue
Terrapins
are terrific with needles
But what does a didgery do?

Bloodhounds
play good rounds of poker
Chihuahuas
do nothing but chew
Poodles
make puddles to paddle in
But what does a didgery do?

A puffin
will stuff in a muffin
A canary
can nearly canoe
Hummingbirds
hum something rotten
But what does a didgery do?

Tapeworms
play tapes while out jogging
Flies
feed for free at the zoo
Headlice
use headlights at night-time
But what does a didgery do?

What does a didgery
What does a didgery
What does a didegeridoo?

Ticklish

When is a
stickleback
ticklish?

When it's
tickled
with a
little stick
of liquorice.

Handfish

Handfish
are grand fish

they swim
about in pairs

hold each other
when they fall in love

and when
they say their prayers.

*   *   *

They tickle
the sea's bare bottom

playful
as little kittens

and when
there's a nip in the ocean

wear brightly
coloured mittens.

Whales

whales
are floating cathedrals
let us rejoice

cavorting mansions
of joy
let us give thanks

divine temples
of the deep
we praise thee

whaleluja!

Cross Porpoises

The porpoises
were looking really cross
so I went over
and talked at them

Soon they cheered up
and swam away
leaving laughter-bubbles
in their wake

It never fails,
talking at cross porpoises.

A Conger Eel

Is there
a longer meal
than a
conger eel?

Old Hippos

Old hippos
   one supposes
have terrible
   colds in the noses

Attracted to these
   nasal saunas
germs build their nests
   in darkest corners

Then hang a sign
   that says politely
(streaming, streaming,
   day and nightly)

'Thank you for havin' us
in your nostrils so cavernous.'

Poor Old Moose

Short-sighted hunters
choose moose

A target as large
as an orphanage wall

The quicker the trigger
the harder they fall

Short-sighted hunters
go home to their wives

Hang hats on the antlers
live short-sighted lives.

Shark in the Park

Ever see
a shark
picnic
in the park?

If he offers
you a bun

run.

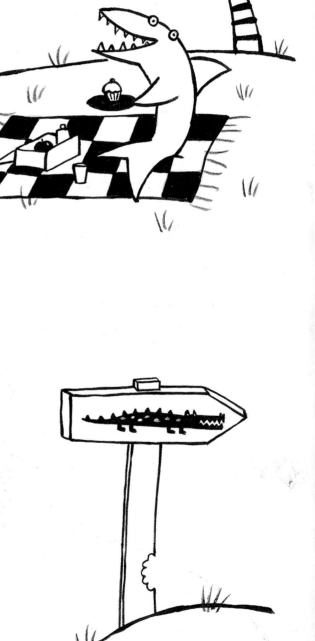

Crocodile Farm

Come wi' me
Down to Crocodile Farm
If you keep your eyes open
You'll come to no harm

There's the old milking shed
Where it's all done by hand
Though we've lost quite a few
As you'll well understand

123

We make crocodile butter
Yoghurt and cream
Though nobody buys it
It's all lumpy and green

High up on the pastures
They're put out to graze
Where they round up the shepherds
And worry them for days

Then we fatten them up
And kill them humanely
The ones we can catch —
They kill us, mainly

But crocodile meat
is an acquired taste
A cross between sewage
And stale salmon paste

So I'm giving up crocodiles
Cos my account's in the red
And starting a farm
For alligators instead.

The Allivator

at the top.

then eat you

his back

ride upon

let you

he will

in a shop

see one

if you

allivator

Beware the

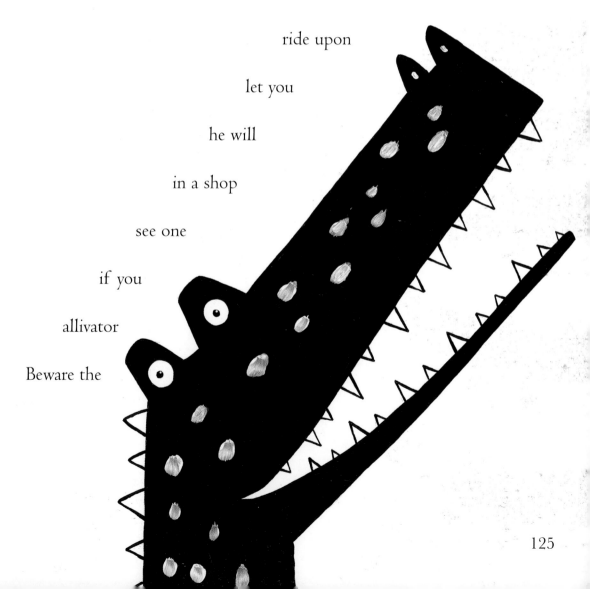

125

An Anaconda

Ever see
an anaconda
drive through town
on a brand-new Honda?

Don't ask him
for a ride

You might end up
inside.

A Water Bison

A
water bison
is what
yer wash
yer face in.

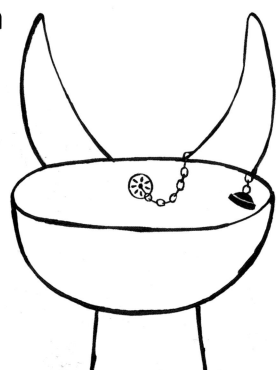

A Teapet

A teapet
I can recommend
to those who need
a loyal friend

Quiet, reliable
he'll never stray
content to sit
on his kitchen tray

Give him water
stroke his spout
say 'thank you'
when the tea comes out.

127

A Catapillow

A catapillow
is a useful pet

To keep
upon your bed

Each night you simply
fluff him up

Then rest
your weary head.

A 13-Amp Slug

A 13-amp slug
you are likely to find
in the garden under a rock

Be careful
how you pick it up

You might get
a nasty shock.

The Brushbaby

The Brushbaby
lives under the stairs
on a diet of dust
and old dog hairs

In darkness, dreading
the daily chores
of scrubbing steps
and kitchen floors

Dreaming of beauty
parlours and stardom
doomed to a life
of petty chardom.

Bookworms

Bookworms
   are the cleverest
of all the worms I know

While others
   meet their fate
on a fisherman's hook as bait

Or churn out silk
   or chew up earth
or simply burn and glow

They loll
   about in libraries
eating words to make them grow

(Vegetarians mainly,
   they are careful
what they eat

Avoiding names
   of animals
or references to meat)

They live
    to ripe old ages
and when it's time to wend

They slip
    between the pages
curl up, and eat 'The End'.

A War Thog

A war thog
is a mercenary beast

Who will show you
no mercy
until you're deceased

Armed to the teeth
with tusks
like scimitars

If you see one
give it
the widest perimeters.

Born to Bugle

He was born to bugle
To be a bugler-boy
Not a teddy bear or a bouncy ball
But a bugle his first toy

He bugled before breakfast
In the bath-tub and in bed
And in between he practised
Bugling on his head

He bugled on his bicycle
He bugled on the bus
At the zoo played boogie-woogie
With a hip hippopotamus

He bugled in Bulgaria
Botswana and Bahrein
Stowed below in cargo
Blowing bugle on a plane

He was born to bugle
Be bugling still today
But a burglar burgled his bugle
and took his breath away

And though we mourn the bugle
We mourn the bugler most
As laid to rest we do our best
To whistle 'The Last Post'.

Bubble Trouble

The trouble with Bobby is bubbles
Been his hobby since he was a boy
When Santa brought him a bubble
One Christmas instead of a toy

Since then he has tried to recapture
The magic of that shimmering sphere
And decided the blowing of bubbles
Would be his chosen career

Fairy Liquid he pours on his cornflakes
Scented soap he spreads on his toast
To be undisputed world champion
'A billion I'll blow!' his proud boast

Golden globes, silver orbs and Belishas
All manner of ball he creates
And with a fair wind behind him
A small Zeppelin our hero inflates

But the trouble with all of his bubbles
Though perfect in every way
Though fashioned with love and attention
(And we're talking a thousand a day)

These incandescent flotillas
These gravitational blips
These would-be orbiting planets
Within seconds of leaving his lips

Go POP! Just like that

Good Mates

There's good mates and bad mates
  'Sorry to keep you waiting' mates
Cheap skates and wet mates
  The ones you end up hating mates
Hard mates and fighting mates
  Witty and exciting mates
Mates you want to hug
  And mates you want to clout
Ones that get you into trouble
  And ones that get you out.

Me and My Shadow

Me and my shadow
Went out to a club last night.
Me and my shadow
Came home just a little tight

At twelve o'clock
We reached the flat
Unlocked the door
Tripped over the mat

Then suddenly noticed
Lying in the spinning hall
The shadow I lay with
Clearly wasn't mine at all

So who's got my shadow
Will the one who's taken it
Please send my shadow
Back because this one is several sizes too big and doesn't fit!

A Gottle of Geer

(To be read aloud without moving the lips)

I an a little wooden dunny
With a hand inside ny gack
How I niss ny daddy and nunny
Now the future's looking glack

Locked all day in a suitcase
I seldon see the sun
I've never tasted lenonade
Or a guttered hot cross gun

The owner takes ne out at night
To sit on his gony knee
He talks a load of ruggish
I think you will agree

Gut the audience go gananas
'Gravo!' 'Gravo!' they cheer
As he drinks a glass of water
And I say: 'A bottle of beer.'

Potato Clock

A potato clock, a potato clock
  Has anybody got a potato clock?
A potato clock, a potato clock
  Oh where can I find a potato clock?

I went down to London the other day
Found myself a job with a lot of pay
Carrying bricks on a building site
From early in the morning till late at night

No one here works as hard as me
I never even break for a cup of tea
My only weakness, my only crime
Is that I can never get to work on time

A potato clock, a potato clock
  Has anybody got a potato clock?
A potato clock, a potato clock
  Oh where can I find a potato clock?

I arrived this morning half an hour late
The foreman came up in a terrible state
'You've got a good job, but you're in for a shock,
If you don't get up at eight o'clock.'

Up at eight o'clock, up at eight o'clock
Has anybody got up at eight o'clock?
Up at eight o'clock, up at eight o'clock
Oh where can I find up at eight o'clock?

Simple Questions

Is a well-wisher
   someone
who wishes at a well?

Is a bad speller
   one
who casts a wicked spell?

Is a shop-lifter
   a giant
who goes around lifting shops?

Is a popsinger
   someone
who sings and then pops?

Is a fly fisherman
    an angler
who fishes for flies?

Is an eye-opener
    a gadget
for opening eyes?

Is a night nurse
    a nurse
who looks after the night?

Who puts it to bed
    and then
turns out the light?

Is a big spender
    a spendthrift
who is exceedingly big?

Is a pig farmer
    really
a land-owning pig?

Is a potholer
    a gunman
who shoots holes in pots?

Does a babysitter
    really
sit on tiny tots?

Is a tree surgeon
    a doctor
made out of wood?

Is a blood donor
    pitta bread
stuffed with blood?

Is a cardsharp
    a craftsman
who sharpens cards?

Who guards women
            when
    a guardsman guards?

Is a batsman
    a man
who is completely bats?

Is a cat burglar
    a thief
who likes stealing cats?

Is a flat tyre
    a tyre
that you keep in a flat?

Is a hat-trick
    a method
of stealing a hat?

Will a pain-killer
    kill you
in terrible pain?

Is a rain hood
    a gangster
who sings in the rain?

Is a tail gunner
    a gunner
with a big long tail?

Do shoppers buy
    giants
in a giant sale?

Does a lightning conductor
    conduct
orchestras fast?

Is a past master
    a master
who has mastered the past?

Is a light bulb
    a bulb
that is as light as a feather?

Does an opera buff
    sing
in the altogether?

Is a slip road
    a road
that is covered in ice?

Are price cuts
    wounds
you get at a price?

Is a waiting room
    a room
that patiently waits?

Is a gatekeeper's
    hobby
collecting gates?

Is a prayer mat
  a carpet
that sings hymns and prays?

Is a horsefly
  a fly
that gallops and neighs?

Does a pony trap
  trap ponies
going to the fair?

Is fire-hose
  stockings
that firemen wear?

Is witchcraft
  jewellery
made by a witch?

Does a battery hen
  cry
when you turn the switch?

Is a scratch team
  so itchy
it scratches?

When a bricklayer
  lays a brick
what hatches?

Is sandpaper
   used
for wrapping up sand?

If you lay down
   your arms
can you still lend a hand?

Is a sick bed
   a bed
that is feeling unwell?

Is a crime wave
   a criminal's
wave of farewell?

Is a cop shop
   a shop
where you can purchase a cop?

Is the last laugh
   the long one
before the big drop?

Is a bent copper
a policeman
who has gone round the bend?

Is the bottom line
the line
on your bottom? The End.

Zombie

I'm a fish out of water
I'm two left feet
On my own and lonely
I'm incomplete

I'm boots without laces
I'm jeans without the zip
I'm lost, I'm a zombie
I'm a dislocated hip.

The Going Pains

Before I could even understand
The meaning of the word 'command'
I've had them. The going pains.

Go to your room
Go to bed
Go to sleep

Twinges that warned of trouble in store
And once in the classroom, the more
I felt them. The going pains.

Go to the back
Go and start again
Go to the Headmaster

From year to year I hear it grow
That unrelenting list of GO.
That bossy word that rhymes with NO
Still can hurt. The going pains.

Go
Go now
Why don't you just go.

A Ring

'Give me a ring,' said Amanda
To the boy she met on a train
'Sure thing,' said Harry, excited
At the thought of seeing her again

So he telephoned next morning
And they chatted till late afternoon
Then she rang back in the evening
And they talked the light off the moon

They talked the hind legs off donkeys
They talked the leaves off the trees
They talked the sheep off the hillsides
They talked the wind off the seas

They talked the colours off rainbows
They talked the carpets off floors
They talked the chimneys off rooftops
They talked the numbers off doors

They talked the laces off trainers
They talked the diamonds off crowns
They talked the skins off bananas
They talked the noses off clowns

They talked the witches off broomsticks
They talked the whiskers off cats
They'd have talked till the Last Trumpet sounded
Had phone bills not dropped on their mats

'Give me a ring,' said Amanda
'Hip hip,' said Harry, 'hooray!'
And with the cash they'd have squandered
Got married the following day.

What She Did

What she did
was really awful
It made me feel quite ill
It was wrong and quite unlawful
I feel queasy still.

What she did
was quite uncalled for
How could she be so cruel?
My friends were all appalled, for
she made me look a fool.

What she did
was out of order
It made me blush and wince
From that instant I ignored her
And haven't spoken since.

What she did
was really rotten.
But what it was
I've quite forgotten.

Joy at the Sound

Joy at the silver birch in the morning sunshine
Joy at the spring-green of its fingertips

Joy at the swirl of cold milk in the blue bowl
Joy at the blink of its bubbles

Joy at the cat revving up on the lawn
Joy at the frogs that leapfrog to freedom

Joy at the screen as it fizzes to life
Joy at The Simpsons, Lisa and Bart

Joy at the dentist: 'Fine, see you next year'
Joy at the school gates: 'Closed'

Joy at the silver withholding the chocolate
Joy at the poem, two verses to go

Joy at the zing of the strings of the racquet
Joy at the bounce of the bright yellow ball

Joy at the key unlocking the door
Joy at the sound of her voice in the hall.

Fame

The best thing
about being famous

is when you walk
down the street

and people turn round
to look at you

and bump into things.

Superman's Little Brother

Being Superman's short-sighted, weedy,
scrawny kid brother isn't easy.
Sticky-fingered toddlers pick fights
with me in misadventure playgrounds.

On beaches, 7-stone weaklings
kick sand in my eyes
vandalize my pies
and thrash me with candyfloss.

They all tell their friends
how they licked Superman ...
(well, not Superman exactly
but his titchy, snotty-nosed, four-eyed little brother.)

Bullied by Brownies
Mugged by nuns
without a doubt, the fun's gone out
of being related to a comic-book hero.

When I grow up I want to marry
Wonderwoman's freckly, podgy little sister.
She's certainly not pretty
She may not be bright
In fact, she's so ordinary
I think we'd get on just right.

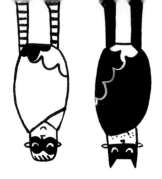

Goodbat Nightman

God bless all policemen
and fighters of crime,
May thieves go to jail
for a very long time.

They've had a hard day
helping clean up the town,
Now they hang from the mantelpiece
both upside-down.

A glass of warm blood
and then straight up the stairs,
Batman and Robin
are saying their prayers.

✳   ✳   ✳

They've locked all the doors
and they've put out the bat,
Put on their batjamas
(They like doing that)

They've filled their batwater-bottles
made their batbeds,
With two springy battresses
for sleepy batheads.

They're closing red eyes
and they're counting black sheep,
Batman and Robin
are falling asleep.

The Figment Tree

I believe in fairies
And each Sunday after tea
At the bottom of the garden
Beneath the figment tree
Alone, I sit and wonder
If they believe in me.

When to Cut Your Fingernails

Cut them on Monday
There's a good week ahead

Cut them on Tuesday
Better go straight to bed

Cut them on Wednesday
You're going to be rich

Cut them on Thursday
You might meet a witch

Cut them on Friday
You'll be walked off your feet

Cut them on Saturday
You're in for a treat

But cut them on Sunday
Without saying a prayer
And your nails will grow
As long as your hair!

Tears For the Tooth Fairy

The Tooth Fairy is crying.
Not tears of pain, but of disappointment.
Yesterday morning,
Not looking where she was flying
She flew straight into a toadstool
And knocked out her front tooth.

So, sleepy at bedtime
She put it under her pillow
Before turning off the light,
Made a wish and fell asleep.
And guess what? You're right.
This morning the tooth was still there!

Gruesome

I was sitting in the sitting room
toying with some toys
When from a door marked: 'GRUESOME'
there came a GRUESOME noise.

Cautiously I opened it
and there to my surprise
A little GRUE lay sitting
with tears in its eyes

'Oh little GRUE please tell me
what is it ails thee so?'
'Well I'm so small,' he sobbed,
'GRUESSES don't want to know'

'Exercises are the answer,
Each morning you must do some'
He thanked me, smiled,
and do you know what?
The very next day he . . . grew some.

Film

Went to the cinema
Friday.
Tried to leave before
the end.

Couldn't get out.
It was a cling film.

Cling-Film

I'm clingy
I cling
to any old thing
a sandwich, a shoe, whatever you bring

I'm clingy
I cling
you can see right through
and when I cling, I cling like glue

I'm clingy
I cling
and I'm coming for you
cling cling cling

Gotcha!

The Scarecrow

The scarecrow is a scary crow
Who guards a private patch
Waiting for a trespassing
Little girl to snatch

Spitting soil into her mouth
His twiggy fingers scratch
Pulls her down on to the ground
As circling birdies watch

Drags her to his hidey-hole
And opens up the hatch
Throws her to the crawlies
Then double locks the latch

The scarecrow is a scary crow
Always out to catch
Juicy bits of compost
To feed his cabbage patch

So don't go where the scarecrows are
Don't go there, Don't go there
Don't go where the scarecrows are
Don't go, Don't go . . .

Don't go where the scarecrows are
Don't go there, Don't go there
Don't go where the scarecrows are
Don't go, Don't go . . .

Don't go where the scarecrows are
Don't go there, Don't go there

161

Only a Dream?

I woke up, and it was only a dream.
With a huge sigh of relief, I got out of bed
and then I saw it, hovering in the corner ...

A skull dripping blood and green slime.
Its eye sockets staring, not at me,
but at some unspeakable horror beyond.

I turned and ran towards the door.
But too late. It slammed shut
locking me in from the outside.

As I tugged at the handle, it broke off
and became white-hot. I dropped it
on the carpet which burst into flames.

The smoke was acrid, burning. I staggered
across the room, hands over my eyes
and collapsed unconscious on the bed.

I woke up and it was only a dream.
With a huge sense of relief I got out of bed
and then I saw it, hovering in the corner ...

Pantomime Poem

'HE'S BEHIND YER!'
chorused the children
but the warning came too late.

The monster leaped forward
and fastening its teeth into his neck,
tore off the head.

The body fell to the floor
'MORE,' cried the children

'MORE, MORE, MORE

MORE

MORE.'

Customer Service

Last Thursday, the telephone
never stopped ringing.
All day. Never stopped.
Even when I answered it.

So I rang British Telecom
and complained. Told them
it was making my head ache
and would they cut it off.

Sure enough, they sent a man
with an axe, the very next day.
(It's dark down here in the cellar
I wish he'd go away.)

I'm a Grown Man Now

I'm a grown man now
Don't easily scare
(if you don't believe me
ask my teddy bear).

Limps

Limps lie around
occasionally in pairs
in wait for someone walking
completely unawares

At the sound of a footstep
they prick up their ears
licking their lips
as the victim appears

They whiplash the foot
as it passes by
then sink in their teeth
as you let out a cry

Holding fast to your ankle
they feed off the pain
as you stumble like someone
dragging a chain

And when at last the doctor
says, 'It's only a sprain'
they've scuttled off cackling
to lie in wait again

The Kleptomaniac

Beware the Kleptomaniac
Who knows not wrong from right
He'll wait until you turn your back
Then steal everything in sight:

The nose from a snowman
(Be it carrot or coal)

The stick from a blindman
From the beggar his bowl

The smoke from a chimney
The leaves from a tree

A kitten's miaow
(Pretty mean you'll agree)

He'll pinch a used teabag
From out of the pot

A field of potatoes
And scoff the whole lot

(Is baby still there,
Asleep in its cot?)

He'll rob the baton
From a conductor on stage

All the books from the library
Page by page

He'll snaffle your shadow
As you bask in the sun

Pilfer the currants
From out of your bun

He'll lift the wind
Right out of your sails

Hold your hand
And make off with your nails

When he's around
Things just disappear

F nnily eno gh I th nk
Th re's one ar und h re!

The Man Who Steals Dreams

Santa Claus has a brother
A fact few people know
He does not have a friendly face
Or a beard as white as snow

He does not climb down chimneys
Or ride in an open sleigh
He is not kind and giving
But cruelly takes away

He is not fond of children
Or grown-ups who are kind
And emptiness the only gift
That he will leave behind

He is wraith, he is silent
He is greyness of steam
And if you're sleeping well tonight
Then hang on to your dream

He is sour, he is stooping
His cynic's cloak is black
And if he takes your dream away
You never get it back

Dreams with happy endings
With ambition and joy
Are the ones that he seeks
To capture and destroy

So, if you don't believe in Santa
Or in anything at all
The chances are his brother
Has already paid a call.

The Tongue-twister

Watch out for the dreaded Tongue-twister
When he pulls on his surgical gloves.
Keep your eyes open, your mouth tightly shut,
Twisting tongues is the thing that he loves.

It's the slippery, squirmy feel of them
As they wriggle like landed fish.
When he pulls and tugs and grapples
You'll gasp and gurgle and wish

That you'd never pulled tongues at teacher
Or a stranger behind their back,
As he twists out your tongue and pops it
Into his bobbling, twisted-tongue sack.

The Sound Collector

A stranger called this morning
Dressed all in black and grey
Put every sound into a bag
And carried them away

The whistling of the kettle
The turning of the lock
The purring of the kitten
The ticking of the clock

The popping of the toaster
The crunching of the flakes
When you spread the marmalade
The scraping noise it makes

The hissing of the frying pan
The ticking of the grill
The bubbling of the bathtub
As it starts to fill

The drumming of the raindrops
On the windowpane
When you do the washing-up
The gurgle of the drain

The crying of the baby
The squeaking of the chair
The swishing of the curtain
The creaking of the stair

A stranger called this morning
He didn't leave his name
Left us only silence
Life will never be the same.

Lullaby

No monsters are hiding under the bed
  I give you my word
The idea of vampires thirsting for blood
  Is plainly absurd .

There are no such things as ghosts I promise
  They're all in the mind
Headless horsemen, hobgoblins and aliens
  All nonsense you'll find

You will not fall under a witch's spell
  You are not Snow White
Nor am I a handsome prince, but still
  A kiss, God bless, good night.

Index of First Lines

A   126

A 13-amp slug   128

a cat mistrusts the sun   87

A catapillow   128

A crab, I am told,   114

A crow is a crow is a crow   106

A domesticated donkey from Slough   109

A ginger tom   88

A little girl called Josephine   97

A millionbillionwillion miles from home   4

A porcupine   113

A potato clock, a potato clock   138

A stranger called this morning   170

A teapet   127

A war thog   131

An advertising whizz-kid   77

'And there goes the bell for the third month   60

Apparently we are all living   83

Before I could even understand   147

Being Superman's short-sighted, weedy,   153

Beware the   125

Beware the Kleptomaniac   166

Bookworms   130

Catfish   116

Come wi' me   123

Cousin Nell   93

Cousin Reggie   92

cuck oo cuck oo cuck   62

Cut the cackle   38

Cut them on Monday   156

Dad, risen and dizzy   43

Despite the cold   75

Don't give your rocking horse   110

Down   72

Ever see an anaconda   126

Ever see a shark   123

every evening after tea   102

Everything touches, life interweaves   82

'Give me a ring,' said Amanda   148

God bless all policemen   154

Goldfish   115

Granny's canary   103

Guess how old I am?   19

Handfish   118

'HE'S BEHIND YER!'   163

He's brilliant at karate   25

He was born to bugle 132

His telescope is beyond repair. 76

I am harum 18

I an a little wooden dunny 137

I believe in fairies 155

I found my sock 44

I give you clean air 79

I like a good poem, 26

I like a nice 53

I love a duck called Jack 108

I polish the dining room table 34

I saw 83

I say I say I say 86

I spend my days 30

I took 40 winks 42

I used to keep 104

I wanna be the leader 12

I want to write a new poem. 33

I was sitting in the sitting room 158

I wish I were a crochet 36

I woke up, and it was only a dream. 162

I'm a fish out of water 146

I'm a grown man now 164

I'm clingy 159

I'm older than my eldest son 23

I'm the most important 9

I've got a cold	44
I've taken to my bed	42
If you are very good I will give you:	20
If you go down the High Street today	58
Im in the botom streme	17
In my field of vision	56
Is a well-wisher	139
Is there	120
It is midnight in the ice rink	70
It wasn't me, Miss, it was 'er, Miss	16
It's a sin	84
Joy at the silver birch in the morning sunshine	151
Last night I heard my pillow talk	40
Last Thursday, the telephone	164
Limps lie around	165
litter	62
Me and my shadow	136
Midnight. A knock at the door.	89
Moany Margaret	100
Mother!	84
Mother, while you were at the shops	66
Mrs Moon	75
My daddy's a lawyer	10
My favourite thing is a pebble	24

My sister had an itch   48

My wife bought a fire guard for the living room 85

No monsters are hiding under the bed   172

No peas for the wicked   55

Oh dear, this poem is very weak   59

Old hippos   121

One evening at supper   52

One morning   105

Our street is dead lazy   68

Peter was awake as soon as daylight sidled into his 96

Pussy pussy puddle cat   88

Said the Water Boatman   112

Santa Claus has a brother   168

Seagulls are eagles   107

Short-sighted hunters   122

Snowman in a field   67

The   73

The best thing   152

The Brushbaby   129

The buns are having a fight   54

The cabbage is a funny veg.   56

The first verse contains a princess   37

The Head of our school	8
The man on the pavement	31
The porpoises	120
The reader of this poem	2
The scarecrow is a scary crow	160
The sound of hounds	111
the sun	74
The sun's too hot and the moon's too cold	33
The Tooth Fairy is crying.	157
The trouble with Bobby is bubbles	134
The writer of this poem	1
There are no grannies in this poem	39
There is a Lollipopman	85
There's a plague around	22
There's good mates and bad mates	135
They're at it again	65
This poem is great.	27
To amuse	105
To be a sumo wrestler	95
Trees are great, they just stand and wait	63
Trees have got it all wrong	64
'twould be nice to be	28
Uncle Terry was a skydiver.	94
Vegetarians are cruel, unthinking people.	57

Waiter, there's a sky in my pie   50

Watch out for the dreaded Tongue-twister   169

watch the words   29

We're a five-car family   80

We're the Mafia cats   90

Went to the cinema   159

whales   119

What I love about school   6

What she did   150

When I played as a kid   48

When I was a child   18

When is a   117

When my sister starts to frown   48

When Raymond Gough joined our class   13

Where am I now when I need me   32

Wherever night falls   71

Who'd be a bottom? Not me.   49

Who's that sailor   78

Why do sheep   109

You couldn't smell your dinner   46